T0207647

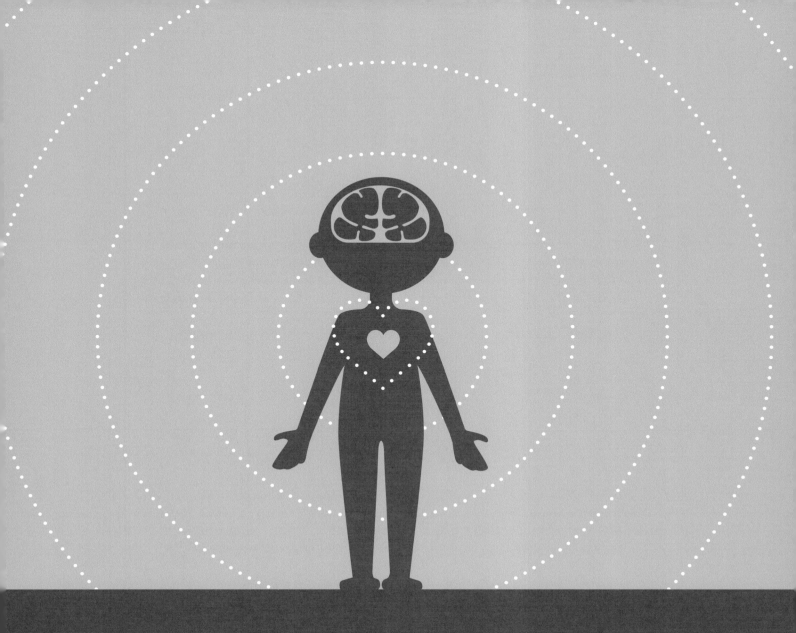

Beginner's Mind Presents:

KIDS BODY CONNECTION

How to Use the Body to Improve Focus and Self Control

Written by Ricardo and Juliana Rodrigues　　　　*Graphics and Illustrations by Rebecca Spin*

Balboa Press books may be ordered through booksellers or by contacting:

Balboa Press
A Division of Hay House
1663 Liberty Drive
Bloomington, IN 47403
www.balboapress.com
844-682-1282

ISBN: 978-1-9822-5505-3 (sc)
ISBN: 978-1-9822-5506-0 (e)

Print information available on the last page.

Balboa Press rev. date: 06/07/2021

There is always room for improvement.

Kids Body Connection (KBC) was envisioned and developed to help children of all body types and all ages, while respecting the unique capabilities of each individual. Think of it as a manual for the human body. Parental influence, popular culture and natural tendencies impact the body's development, but we can always affect future development by incorporating the KBC practice into our daily routine. The four pillars of fitness (Posture, Flexibility, Balance, and Agility) create a safe and strong foundation, so the body can adapt and learn many different skills throughout a lifetime. Approach the body gently but be persistent and assertive when it comes to proper form. Deal with challenges as they present themselves, in the moment. Something as simple as breathing with conscious awareness can resolve some of the most complex challenges. With patience and a positive attitude, you can help your child embrace new habits.

Table of Contents

1

About the Program

Kids Body Connection (KBC) was developed to teach children how to use their body as a tool for everyday life. We start by influencing a Beginner's mind Mindset, open to learn and open to grow. The 15-minute program is designed with four parts.

Part 1: Conscious Body Flow (CBF), where a positive relationship with gravity is developed and applied. Good form is a great way to start the day.

Part 2: Conscious Breathing Exercises (CBE). Here we practice two rounds of 20 to 30 breaths with retention. Breathing practices allow children to pause and feel the feelings inside their body, allowing for a greater understanding of self.

Part 3: Body Connection Exercises (BCE). Here we focus on our four Pillars of Fitness: Posture, Flexibility, Balance, and Agility – the most foundational practice for human growth and development for everyday living activities.

Part 4: A Moment of Silence. For three minutes, all children sit together and pause to feel the sensations inside their body transitioning into a growth mindset, ready to learn.

Kids Body Connection is a golden program designed to elevate human potential from an early age. Imagine if you had learned about your body and how to use it while at school. KBC is changing the way children interact, understand, and act toward themselves and others. Together we can integrate this simple, educational, timeless, and fun program in all schools.

How to use this book:

The Kids Body Connection is a manual, and our intention is for you to use this knowledge consistently. Making it into a routine is what is going to allow the efficacy of this program to be revealed. Start twice a week and gradually increase to up to five times per week. Practice KBC before or after the bell rings (start of class/recesses/any sports or physical education practice); this 15-minute practice will encourage a mindset of growth and openness to learning. This program can be practiced by groups or individuals at critical moments like when focus and self-control are lost. It is designed to be self-applied and taught daily to evolve into a healthy habit. It is highly recommended for teachers, educators, parents, coaches, personal trainers, and caregivers. Use it for yourself and with your friends. Enjoy your practice!

2
Fundamentals of Coaching Children

These are the five core values that must be applied when dealing with the human body.

The human body is delicate, yet also resilient and strong. Everyone is different and these five core values are what make us similar and able to educate children at different levels, customizing to their individual capabilities. When these core values are explained and applied while exercising, consistent progress will be made. Keep clear communication, and a healthy student-coach relationship will be developed!

"First, do no Harm." –Hippocrates
The body is the ultimate healer and understanding how it works is crucial to taking better care of it. Furthermore, enhancing the body's capabilities is always an excellent path to health, assisting in the prevention of future harm through understanding.

Pain is the body's language.

Everybody reacts differently to pain. Understanding how something feels helps the mind to direct body parts correctly. Allow participants to understand their body's language by teaching them to grade their levels of discomfort, so they can make inferences in the future on their own.

Take a gentle approach!

The body fights back when it is forced. With gentle but constant nudges in the right direction, progress can be made in healthy ways. Teach forgiveness for mistakes made in the past and focus on the present path to improvement.

It's not as easy as it looks.

Each person can be at a different stage of learning and physical health in their life, and effort is always required to achieve what you want. Practice makes progress, so keep on going!

There's always room for improvement!

This self-belief motivates the mind to keep putting in the effort and progress organically. Celebrate every little victory to make the journey more enjoyable!

3
Conscious Body Flow

The **Conscious Body Flow (CBF)** is a mental tool developed to control and direct the body parts into alignment and balance. By imagining a cyclical wave around the body, going up along the front and down along the back, CBF helps to correct, connect, and lift the body for better performance during any movement. Apply it when standing, sitting, and practicing any sports or activities.

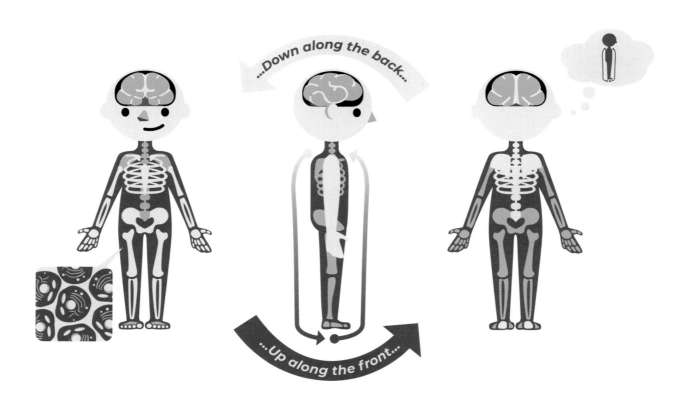

...Down along the back...

...Up along the front...

How to Apply Conscious Body Flow:

1. Stand tall

2. Press your heels into the ground

3. Start lifting from the arches of your feet

4. Lift your kneecaps and hip bones up

5. Hollow your belly in and up (like preparing to receive a cannon ball!)

6. Lift your chest up toward your collar bone

7. Focus on the backs of your shoulders and press them down

8. Continue going down your back to the bottom of your spine

9. Connect with the back of your legs all the way down to your heels

10. Continue lifting up along the front of your body and pressing down along the back of your body (keep it fluid, like an imaginary circle!)

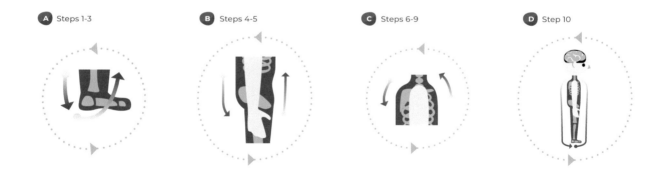

A Steps 1-3   B Steps 4-5   C Steps 6-9   D Step 10

Focus on the feelings- control the flow of the wave!

If your body is not flowing (like aches or tightness), back off, take a moment, and reset your body. Then try again!

Conscious Breathing Exercises

Conscious Breathing is a natural way to wake up one's mind-body synergy. This combined force of thought (mind) and matter (body) produces a powerful outcome by integrating real-time feeling with the understanding of how the breath feels inside the body.

Ideally, conscious breathing should be practiced twice a day, but should definitely be practiced at least once a day. It can be used as needed to regain focus and relieve stress.

Benefits of Conscious Breathing

- Developing the good habit of conscious breathing will improve self-awareness, focus and self-control.
- When provided with a calm internal environment, the body can easily maintain a state of wellbeing.

How to Apply Conscious Breathing:

1. Lying or sitting in a comfortable position, put your hands on your belly

2. Start breathing continuously for 2 minutes

3. Emphasize the inhale and expand your belly as if filling up a balloon with air

4. Exhale until your belly returns to a normal position

5. On the last exhale (after 2 minutes of breathing), hold your breath for as long as you can (Fig. B)

6. When you feel the need to breathe, take a big breath IN and hold (Fig. C) for 10 seconds (count on your fingers), exhale and release

7. Regroup and check in (if more than one person is participating)

8. Repeat the process one more time.

| **A** 2 min breathing | **B** Last breath out and hold | **C** Breathe in, hold 10 sec | **D** Repeat steps B and C |

Start by holding your breath for 30 seconds, then for 45 seconds, and finally for 1 minute. Keep track of the retentions!

Let the sensations happen!

Feelings to look for:

Feeling at ease

Slight lightness in the head

The body feels looser

Tingling in the hands

Use the scale below to assess the physical and psychological level of effort of the child. The goal is to guide them toward the **Optimal Effort Zone.** If the child is performing in the minimum effort zone, encourage the child to increase the effort to the optimal zone. If the child shows signs of physical or psychological struggle, help them reduce the effort or stop the activity.

1-4: Minimum Effort Zone   **5-7:** Optimal Effort Zone

7: Threshold   **8-10:** Injury Effort Zone

Effort Scale

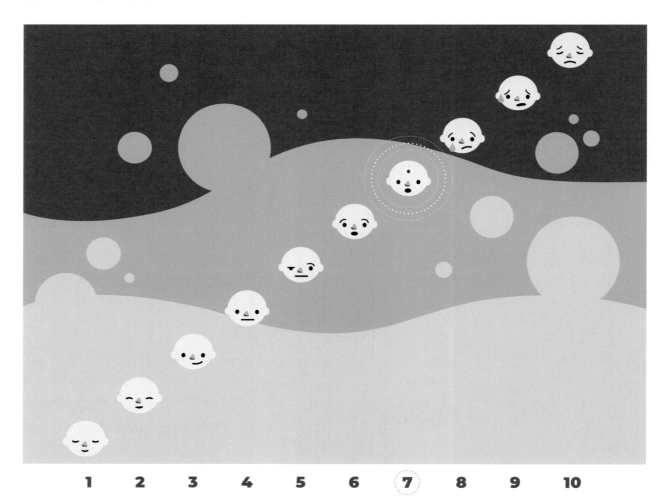

5

Body Connection Exercises

Integrating All Your Body Parts Into Your Body

Practice correct **Posture** and you will produce the right hormones as well as greater attention span, stamina, and self-confidence.

Practice **Flexibility** and you will ensure your range of motion is being stimulated in many directions. Mobility allows us to operate in a more relaxed state of mind.

Practice **Balance** and all your skills will improve. The quality of your walking will improve, and the chance of falling will decrease.

Agility is the pinnacle of them all. It requires good Posture, Flexibility, and Balance to achieve Agility - the ability to move efficiently, quickly, and skillfully.

We've created a script for you to read out loud so the children can follow along with the right timing and rhythm. The script begins on page 12 and continues through page 25, denoted by musical notes on the green pages.

Kids Body Connection Daily Script

Hey you

It's time to connect to your

body

Close your eyes

and imagine

you are sitting in a director's

chair

Make yourself comfortable

You are now

the director of your own body

When you focus on your body

you can direct the flow

to where your body parts go

It's simple

get ready

action

Lift your core up and keep it up

Press your shoulders down and

keep them down

Lift your chest up and keep up

the flow

Press your heels down

And down the flow goes

Now put it all together like one

big O

Connect your body flow

Keep it going

That's great self-control

Along the back

down you direct

Stay up along the front

and into the flow you will get

Everything in your body

is you

Let's start from your heart

It is your pumping body part

Your lungs will work in synergy

converting oxygen into energy

Place your hands on your belly

the core of it all

You are going to make it

big and small

Now breathe air in

make your belly big

Let the air out

Make it small

Focus on yourself

Breathe fully in

Let it out

Not fully out

Breathe fully in

Let it go

Keep on breathing

You're going to feel

lightness in your head

Looseness in your body

Tingling in your hands

It is all normal

Focus on those feelings

Breathe in, let go

Breathe in, let go

Make the air flow

Now breathe air in

Make your belly big

Let the air out

Make your belly small

Breathe fully in

Let it out

Not fully out

Now fully in

Let it go

Keep on breathing

Focus on those feelings

Breathe in, let go

Breathe in, let go

Make the air flow

When I say hold

you are going to let the air out

and hold

Let's make the last five breaths

Count

All together

Breathe in deep

Let it out

Fully in

Let it out

3 more to go

Fully in

Let it go

Fully in

Let it go

Last one

Make it count

Fully in

Gently out

and hold

No more breathing

You are now full of energy

Trust

you have enough oxygen in

your body

Hold for as long as you can

When you feel the need to

breathe again

Go ahead and take a big breath

in

and hold it again

Keep the breath in

Count 10 Second on your

fingers

Now gently let the air out

and feel the sensations inside

your body

Now let's start round 2

as a team

All together

Breathe in

Let the air out

Focus on yourself

Breath fully in

Let it out

Not fully out

Now fully in

Let it go

Keep on breathing

You're going to feel

lightness in your head

Looseness in the body

Tingling in your hands

It is all normal

Focus on those feelings

Breathe in, let go

Breathe in, let go

Make the air flow

Now breathe air in

Make your belly big

Let the air out

Make your belly small

Breathe fully in

Let it out

Not fully out

Now fully in

Let it go

Keep on breathing

Focus on those feelings

Breathe in, let go

Breathe in, let go

Make the air flow

When I say hold

You are going you let the air out

and hold

Let's make the last five breaths

Count

All together

Breathe in deep

Let it out

Fully in

Let it out

3 more to go

Fully in

Let it go

Fully in

Let it go

Last one

Make it count

Fully in

Gently out

and hold

No more breathing

You are now full of energy

Trust

you have enough oxygen in

your body

Hold for as long as you can

When you feel the need to

breathe again

Go ahead and take a big breath

in

and hold it again

Keep the breath in

Count 10 seconds on your

fingers

Now gently let the air out

and feel the sensations inside

your body

Now as a team

All together

Breathe in

Gently out

Slowly breathe normally

Enjoy this moment

It is time to connect all your

body parts

into your body

make your body strong like the

earth...

Let's begin your posture exercise: *Surfboard*

With your hands pressed on the table

Spread your fingers like a starfish

Extend your arms - shoulders over hands

Extend your body long like a surfboard

for 30 seconds

Get ready, set, go

Stay strong and long

Breathe normally

Core up - chest up - shoulders down - heels down

Lift it up along the front

Press it down along the back

(repeat x 2)

10 9 8 7 6 5 4 3 2 1

You have completed the surfboard exercise

Great effort!

All together

Move your body like water, fluid and flowing...

Posture: Surfboard

Level 1   **Level 2**   **Level 3**

Follow proper form instructions for all levels.
Time: 30 seconds

1. Press hands firmly into the surface

2. Pointing index fingers forward

3. Shoulders over wrists

4. Neck straight, eyes looking at your fingers, imagine there's a string pulling up on you from the middle of your head

5. Chest up, shoulders down and back

6. Cannonball core, belly button up and in

7. Energy moving down the back to your heels

8. Press toes gently into the ground

9. Breathe consciously

10. Full inhale, up along your front; Exhale, down along your back

Let's begin your flexibility
exercise: **Star X**

Stand tall, extend your arms
and legs wide like a star

For 1 minute rotate your upper
body to the left

Right arm should be in front of
your body and

left arm in back

Now reach down to your
left foot

Come back up

Rotate your body to the right

Left arm should be in front of
your body and right arm in back

Now reach down to your
right foot

Come back up

Stay fluid like water

Breathe

Core up

Chest up

Shoulders down

Heels down

Up along the front

Down along the back

10 9 8 7 6 5 4 3 2 1

You have completed the
Star X exercise

Now you can move strong and
fluid like water

How do you feel? Close your
eyes and check in

Can you direct the conscious
body flow?

ⅠⅠ *Flexibility:* Star "X"

Start with the CBF visualization.

Time: 1 minute

1. Wide stance with your legs wider than your hips, align your second toe with your heel

2. Press down through your heels, lift up through your arches

3. Lift kneecaps up

4. Lift cannonball core and chest up

5. Extend arms out with your palms facing up, keep shoulders down

6. Visualize the string pulling up on you from the middle of your head to maintain a straight spine. Keep your core up and hips straight!

7. Rotate your whole upper body and reach your right hand down towards your left foot

8. Come back up to standing

9. Rotate your your whole upper body and reach your left hand down towards your right foot

10. Repeat from side to side maintaining a steady momentum

Lift your body lightly like air

Let's begin

Balance exercise: **_Pogo Stick_**

For 1 minute

Stand tall on your right foot

Lift your Core up

Lift your left knee up

Balance lightly and strong like

air

If you lose your balance, it's

okay

Use the flow

And you will find

the way

Up along the front

Down along the back

Up Along the front

Down along the back

Press your heels down

Lift your core up

Press your shoulders down

Lift your chest up

Press your heels down

Lift your core up

Press your shoulders down

Lift your chest up

10 9 8 7 6 5 4 3 2 1

Switch legs and stand tall on

your left foot

Lift your Core up

lift your right knee up

Balance lightly and strong like

air

If you lose your balance it's okay

Use the flow

And you will find

the way

Up along the front

Down along the back

Up Along the front

Down along the back

Press your heels down

Lift your core up

Press your shoulders down

Lift your chest up

Press your heels down

Lift your core up

Press your shoulders down

Lift your chest up

10 9 8 7 6 5 4 3 2 1

Tiiime!

You have completed the Pogo

Stick exercise

▥ *Balance:* Pogo Stick

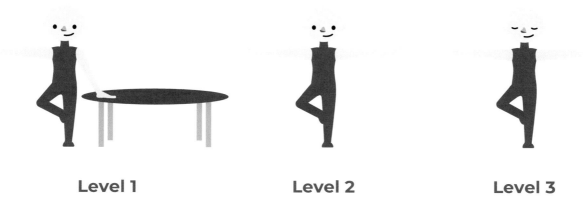

| Level 1 | Level 2 | Level 3 |

Start by visualizing the CBF.
Time: 1 minute per side

1. Press both feet together on the ground.

2. Cannonball (belly button in and up)

3. Open arms wide palms facing up

4. Eyes looking forward.

5. Focus on a still object

6. Posture up

7. Lift your right knee up and flex your foot

8. Imagine the string pullling up on you from the middle of your head to keep your spine straight

9. Lift up along your front, press down along your back (hold for 1 minute)

10. Repeat on the other side

By using the conscious body

flow you can balance like a Pro

You are now ready

Your body has the energy and

speed

To Move fast like Fire

Warm up your engine

Move your arms with your legs

Check your flow

with self-control

keep it soft

Let's begin Agility exercise:

Hot Hot, Hot Hot

For 1 minute

Step your right foot out

and Step your left foot out

Step your right foot in

Step your left foot in

Synchronize your arms with

your legs

Out, out - in, in

Up along the front

and down along the back

Out, out - in, in

Breathe

Hot hot, hot hot

Light and fast like fire

Hot hot, hot hot

Super speed

Hot hot, hot hot

Starting to tame the fire

Hot hot, hot hot

Focus and self-control

Out, out - in, in

Breathe fully in

Out, out - in, in

Keep on moving

10 9 8 7 6 5 4 3 2 1

Out, out - in, in

Can you control your fire?

Out, out - in, in

Breathe

Hot hot, hot hot

Light and fast like fire again

Hot hot, hot hot

Super speed

Hot hot, hot hot

10 9 8 7 6 5 4 3 2 1

Tiiime!

Bring your focus to your body

How are you feeling?

You have completed the hot

hot, hot hot exercise

IV *Agility:* "Hot, Hot, Hot, Hot"

Time: 30 seconds

Pretend that the ground is hot, so the child quickly lifts their feet off the ground instead of stomping down and getting "burned" by the imaginary heat. Inspire the children to build speed with great posture, freedom of motion, and synchronization of the arms and legs.

1. Stand with feet wider than hips with a circle or an imaginary circle on the ground between your feet.

2. Step your right foot in, then step your left foot in

3. Step your right foot out, then step your left foot out

4. Progressively increase your speed

5. Practice CBF - Lift up along the front of your body. Press down along your back.

6. Synchronize your arms and legs so that when your left foot moves, your right arm swings up while your left arm goes back, and vice versa.

7. Keep posture up straight, and stay light on your feet!

On the next round of 30 seconds have the children start with the opposite side; left foot in, right foot in, left foot out, right foot out.

A Moment of Silence

Now for the time we have all been waiting for. Time to put aside the physical effort, and observe how the inside of the body feels at this moment. This is a positive way to reward the mind for challenging the body. The body parts that are still hyperactive have an opportunity to disengage, and let go.

Set up:

Sit or lay down comfortably with the spine straight. You will hold this position for three minutes.

If you are sitting: Sit with legs crossed, or with knees together sitting on your heels. Put your hands on your knees, and keep posture up.

If you are laying down: Keep your spine long, with your legs relaxed. Let your toes fall to the side.

You have the power to control your fire

find a comfortable position

Use your focus and self-control

by directing your

conscious body flow

Take the healthy path

Control your conscious breath

Connect all body parts with balance

Let's begin with

A Moment of Silence

We will start in 3,2,1 ...

You may now close your eyes.

(The children will now engage in three minutes of silent meditation. After three minutes, begin with the script as written to the right.)

All together

Deep breath In

Raise your arms up

Let the air go

Bring your arms down

Once again

Deep breath in

Raise your arms up

Let the air out

Bring your arms down

Your body is fully connected

Go back to your table

Your kids body connection

practice was great!

You have improved your focus and self-control.

7
Conscious Body Corrections

There is no such a thing as perfection, which means there is always room for improvement. Overthinking or not being in the moment are the most common causes of restricting progress and increasing pain. Use the **Conscious Body Corrections** to identify and gently correct the children's performance.

❶ *Conscious Body Flow Corrections*

Too much thinking

Excess effort focused on one body part

Not feeling the flow

II *Conscious Breathing Corrections*

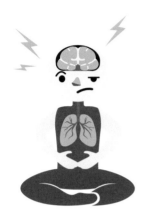  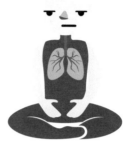

**Too much
thinking**

**Too much effort
on the exhale**

**Not breathing
consciously**

III *Posture*

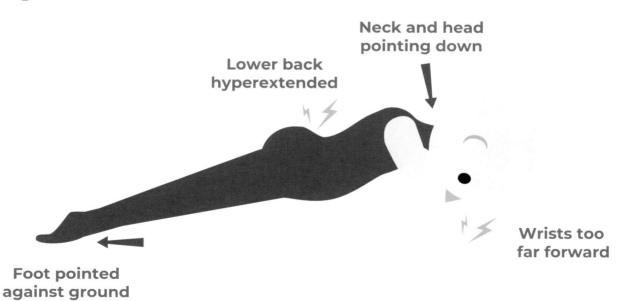

**Neck and head
pointing down**

**Lower back
hyperextended**

**Wrists too
far forward**

**Foot pointed
against ground**

IV Flexibility

**Too much effort
in one place**

Not breathing

Too loose

V Balance

**Too much
thinking**

Not breathing

Too rigid

Agility

**Too much
thinking**

**Not doing
the pattern**

Heavy feet

Head down

Understanding Children's Capabilities

A capability is when a child can perform an activity without signs of physical and psychological struggle. These are two of the most distinct characteristics that you may find.

The Careful Child (Cat)

When trying something new, the Careful Cat may show signs of struggle. This child will carefully observe to acquire new information before attempting new things. In the meantime, they are improving their patience, focus and energy output. They must be encouraged to practice activities constantly, little by little. You will notice their incremental progress, until they can feel the physical capability on their own.

The Carefree Child (Pup)

The Carefree Pup will have a good time no matter what. These explorers love to show off their capabilities, but the catch is that they are not necessarily using the correct form or performing skillfully. Their capabilities will increase or decrease based on how much their body can handle the abuse (incorrect form). A Carefree Child may need a bit of taming. With calm assistance you can guide them to use the four elements (Posture, Flexibility, Balance, and Agility), and help them become aware of what feels right and wrong. With patience and practice they will develop graceful skills.

Kinesthetic Intelligence Scale

The body is a complex organism. Many of our most important physical abilities were developed when logic wasn't even a factor. Necessity and desire got us to crawl, stand, walk, and so on. The **Kinesthetic Intelligence Scale** is a great tool to help you and your students identify the starting point of their physical abilities, and set goals to improve upon them.

Levels	Current physical ability	Necessary Breakthrough	If Action is not Taken	How to Improve
Level I	Unable to perform	Acceptance; Beginner's Mind Mindset is active	No progress will be made	Need constant physical assistance to perform
Level II	Unable to perform without assistance	Building self confidence	Will get stuck in transition between understanding and performing	Conditioning at high repetition with assistance until able to move independently
Level III	Able to perform independently	Intention becoming action	Old patterns can take over; must think to be able to improve	Incorporating the correct pattern of movement until it becomes part of the routine
Level IV	Able to perform independently and apply Kinesthetic Intelligence Scale	Total movement control, feeling of effortlessness	Old patterns will return	Appreciating the benefits, incorporating KIS into lifestyle

This program was inspired by various scientific studies of the Human Body. Following are the references applied:

Dr. Amy J. C. Cuddy, PhD

TED Talk, "Your Body Language May Shape Who You Are" (2012)

Brian Dorfman, Kinesiologist

Flexibility Training, Stretch Strengthen Recovery (2002)

Carol Dweck, PhD

Mindset (2007)

Gil Heddley, PhD

What's the Fuzz?! (1995)

Jon Kabat-Zinn, PhD

Mindfulness for Beginners (2016)

Thomas Myers, Structural Integration

Myofascial Meridians for Manual & Movement Therapists (2014)

Neil Shubin, PhD

The Universe Within: The Deep History of the Human Body (2013)

Wim Hof, The Iceman

The Way of The Iceman (2017)

Testimonials for KBC

"Juliana is a tremendous asset to our staff and students. We highly recommend her and her expertise to those folks interested in her program."

-Kimberly Eurich, Elementary School Assistant at Torrey Pines Elementary School

"Juju is very committed, passionate and energetic. The students connected to her and enjoyed learning... I recommend Kids Body Connection for all students."

-Sarah Ott, Principal at Torrey Pines Elementary School

Testimonial from various Teachers and Parents from Torrey Pines Elementary School in La Jolla California:

"KBC has been excellent for our daughter. She loves it and it helps in all aforementioned points. We would love to have the KBC in the next few years as well."

"Thank you for sharing your time and knowledge. It was a wonderful experience for all and the students loved Tuesdays and Fridays!"

"I've appreciated Miss JuJu's generosity in providing my students (and me!) with the opportunity to learn about our bodies."

"I really appreciate the program. So many kids cannot regulate their emotions or find ways to calm themselves and just take a break and this has allowed them to practice it when they normally wouldn't on their own. I believe patterns we can form with them will stick if they continue the practice."

"I LOVE the program and cannot thank Juju enough for her two visits a week. It brings focus, movement, calming and being in touch with their bodies and how they feel which helps the daily routines and transitions."

Various elementary school students' feedback from 2017, 2018, and 2019:

"Dear Ms. Juju, I am now very good at my posture. Thank you."

"Thank you for teaching us wonderful poses and self control, you taught me a lot."

"I like the surfboard and I love the moment of silence."

"I have a lot of fun when you teach us."

"Thank you for teaching us how to control our body. My favorite exercise is Star X because it makes my hips strong."

"My favorite part is the moment of silence because it is peaceful."

"Thank you for teaching us HotHot because it's fast."

"I like breathing because we need to breathe to live."

"Dear Ms. Juju, I like silly faces."

About the Authors

Ricardo Rodrigues is a Fitness Coach for humans aged 3 years old to 98 years old. He is the founder of the proprietary Beginner's Mind Method, and the creator of the Kids Body Connection Program. Ricardo has studied, applied, and tested many fitness models, training methods, body movements, and fascial manipulation. He has competed in 11 Ironman Championships, eight Half Ironmans, and 15 full Marathons. Combining half marathons, Xterra Triathlons, Biathlons, and most recently Brazilian Jiu Jitsu competitions, he has completed over 500 competitive events. Ricardo's dedication to his work through keen observation and pragmatic application inspired him to develop his own proprietary method while assisting, training, and educating in his private practice. His work has been validated by his long-standing clientele, who have trusted their family members and friends to his care for the past 17 years. It is a mutually collaborative system where his coaching skills assist individuals of all ages to understand their body and its optimal function.

Juju Rodrigues is the co-creator and presenter of the Kids Body Connection Program. She is the apprentice to Ricardo Rodrigues at Beginner's Mind Method. As a Beginner's Mind coach, Juju has been able to study, apply, and test the proprietary method on various fitness models with successful results. She is an advocate in the health and wellness industry with focus on the joy of movement and breathing exercises for everyday practice. In her youth, Juju was a gymnast, participating in local competitions and presentations. After the passing of her father (her coach), she explored the art of Jazz dance. She then moved into Brazilian Capoeira, which allowed her the mixture of movements and freedom of range of motion for the ultimate self-expression. Juju has more than 500 hours of Yoga Practice, and 300 hours in lectures with focus on breath work. She has studied, practiced, and finished the 10-week Iceman training program. Juju is currently leading the Kids Body Connection social movement to teach young humans how to use their bodies as a tool to improve focus and self-control.

About this Book

It's time to teach young humans at schools how to be aware of their bodies. We as parents, teachers, and caregivers understand how important and relieving it is when a child matures and starts gaining more self-control and focus. Self-awareness is a fundamental part of growth. When a human behaves without self-awareness, it is easy to become erratically out of control, out of focus, and irritable. This ultimately discourages a learning mindset.

Kids Body Connection is a simple, 5-step guided daily practice to improve self-awareness and teach methods for centering the body. The program includes breathing techniques for mind-body synergy, exercises for body-conscious movement, and more. By applying the practice of the four elements of Posture, Flexibility, Balance, and Agility, Kids Body Connection will help to stimulate and encourage an optimal mindset for growth, strong athleticism, and longevity.

Printed in the United States
by Baker & Taylor Publisher Services